By Donna Longo
Illustrated by Luciana Navarro Powell

Glenview, Illinois • Boston, Massachusetts • Chandler, Arizona •
Upper Saddle River, New Jersey

ISBN 13: 978-0-328-47232-1
ISBN 10:   0-328-47232-8

2 3 4 5 6 7 8 9 10 V008 13 12 11 10

We've planned a grand parade,
a super celebration.

Our school and all our classes will honor this great nation. **I am so proud!**

3

So much to do, so little time.
There's so much preparation.

'Zip' Our class pet

Gather 'round, one and all.
This takes cooperation!
I am so proud!

5

We have three precious hours
to whip up our creation.

It's a symbol of our pride
to honor our great nation.
I am so proud!

Dip brushes one by one,
swish-swish along the border.

Paint stripes so straight and true,
red, white, red, white, in order.
I am so proud!

Mix buckets of true blue.
Splish-splash! It's like our sky.

Ms. Vogel lends a hand
with spots that are too high.
I am so proud!

11

Fifty white stars twinkle
on a background, oh, so blue.

12

Just like our nation's flag
that waves for me and you!
I am so proud!

Little fingers—one, two, three—
crunch crinkly paper roses.

All the flowers look so real.
We sniff them with our noses!
I am so proud!

Our float is done. Hooray!
Our flags are side-by-side.

We all stand at attention.
Ms. Vogel is our guide.
I am so proud!

Tap-tap the rhythm sticks!
Crash the cymbals loudly!

Plink-plink the xylophone!
March with us, oh, so proudly!

We've tackled this big job
With true cooperation.

Ms. Vogel's Class

It takes so many hands
to build a special nation.

We are so proud!

22

Flag Facts

Do you have a nickname? The United States flag does! It's "Old Glory."

What do we call the flag when we sing about it? It's "The Star-Spangled Banner."

Wow! Fifty white stars decorate the flag. Each star stands for one of the fifty states in our United States. Which state do you live in?

Look! There are thirteen stripes on the United States flag. They stand for our first thirteen colonies. Count seven red stripes and six white ones. Which color comes first?